3D OBJECTS

Discovering Cylinders

Nancy Furstinger and John Willis

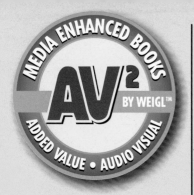

AV² provides enriched content that supplements and complements this book
Weigl's AV² books strive to create inspired learning and engage young minds
in a total learning experience.

Your AV² Media Enhanced books come alive with...

Audio
Listen to sections of
the book read aloud.

Key Words
Study vocabulary, and
complete a matching
word activity.

Video
Watch informative
video clips.

Quizzes
Test your knowledge.

Embedded Weblinks
Gain additional information
for research.

Slide Show
View images and
captions, and prepare
a presentation.

Try This!
Complete activities and
hands-on experiments.

... and much, much more!

Go to **www.av2books.com**,
and enter this book's
unique code.

BOOK CODE

S286495

AV² by Weigl brings you media
enhanced books that support
active learning.

Published by AV² by Weigl
350 5th Avenue, 59th Floor
New York, NY 10118
www.av2books.com

Library of Congress Cataloging-in-Publication Data

Names: Furstinger, Nancy, author. | Willis, John, 1989-, author.
Title: Discovering cylinders / Nancy Furstinger and John Willis.
Description: New York, NY : AV2 by Weigl, [2016] | Series: 3D objects |
   Includes bibliographical references and index.
Identifiers: LCCN 2016005638 (print) | LCCN 2016013991 (ebook) | ISBN
   9781489649805 (hard cover : alk. paper) | ISBN 9781489649812 (soft cover :
   alk. paper) | ISBN 9781489649829 (Multi-user ebk.)
Subjects: LCSH: Cylinder (Mathematics)--Juvenile literature. | Geometry,
   Solid--Juvenile literature.
Classification: LCC QA491 .F8656 2016 (print) | LCC QA491 (ebook) | DDC
   516.156--dc23
LC record available at https://lccn.loc.gov/2016005638

Printed in the United States of America in Brainerd, Minnesota
1 2 3 4 5 6 7 8 9 0 20 19 18 17 16

082016
210716

Project Coordinator: John Willis   Art Director: Terry Paulhus

CONTENTS

FINDING YOUR RHYTHM

You come to music class with your brand-new drum. Try out different sounds by banging the drum with sticks, mallets, and your hands. Count out loud and play a steady beat, or drum with wild **rhythms**.

Drums are usually cylinder-shaped, no matter how big or small they are.

After music, it is lunchtime. You packed a can of juice to drink. Did you notice how the shape of the drum matches the shape of the can? Both of these shapes are **cylinders**.

Many different containers are cylinder-shaped. Can you name some?

WHAT DOES A CYLINDER LOOK LIKE?

There are cylinders all over. Cylinders are not flat. They have three **dimensions**. Flat shapes, like a circle, have only two dimensions, length and width. Flat shapes can also be called plane shapes or 2D shapes.

Shapes that have three dimensions are called **3D** shapes. A cylinder has three dimensions we can measure. These are length, width, and height. 3D shapes are also called solid shapes.

Many writing instruments, such as chalk, are shaped like skinny cylinders.

The little ripples on the sides of a tin can make the can stronger, so it is harder to crush.

HOW DO WE TELL IF A SHAPE IS A CYLINDER?

Look closely. A cylinder has two flat **faces**. These faces are two-dimensional flat **surfaces**.

The two flat, round faces, also called **bases**, are found on each end. If we trace around one of the cylinder's bases, we will draw a circle.

A cylinder has both flat and curved surfaces. The third surface of a cylinder connects the two circle-shaped bases. It looks like a tube. This curved surface has straight sides. If we remove this face and lay it flat, it will form a rectangle.

Cylinders can be tall, short, wide, or skinny.

PARTS OF A CYLINDER

Cylinders have two bases. Each base is shaped like a circle.

base or face

curved surface

CYLINDERS AT THE STORE

Now you know how to spot a cylinder. You can see this 3D shape in everyday objects, even when shopping. Load up your shopping cart with healthy food. Get a bag of pasta tubes. Find your favorite strawberry yogurt. Toss in a big can of vegetable juice and six more cans of alphabet soup. Do not forget rolls of paper towels. What other items can you find in cylinder-shaped containers?

Later, you visit the craft store. You need supplies for art projects. Tiny glass bottles hold colorful beads. You can use the beads to fill a homemade **kaleidoscope**. Bright yarn winds around long spools. Colored pencils come packed in a plastic case. Add a glue stick and a can of spray paint to your cart. So many things have a cylinder shape.

> Many different kinds of pasta are cylinder-shaped, such as rigatoni, penne, and cannelloni.

CYLINDERS AT PLAY

Cylinders can also be very fun. Most playgrounds have tunnel tubes that you can crawl, slide, or walk through. Some of these tunnels are made of rope. Use your hands to help you while the tunnel sways back and forth. When you reach the end of the tunnel, shoot down the slide.

You can make a fun tunnel playground for a pet mouse or gerbil. Save all of your empty paper towel cardboard tubes. Cut slits around the ends of the tubes to join them together. Your pet will have hours of fun playing in the tunnel system. As a bonus, you will also be recycling.

Many slides are shaped like a full cylinder, or a cylinder that has been cut in half.

CYLINDERS IN MACHINES

Cylinders also work hard inside different machines. Rolls of paper spin off of a machine onto a **reel** in a paper factory. A huge cylinder on a steamroller flattens new roads.

Smaller machines with this 3D shape also help us work. A rolling pin makes it easy for us to roll out and flatten dough for pizza or cookies. A paint roller allows you to paint your bedroom walls your favorite color.

Paint rollers are only one kind of cylinder-shaped tool. Can you think of any other tools that are cylinder-shaped?

DIGGING THE EURO TUNNEL

What did engineers use to dig the Euro Tunnel that connects Great Britain with France under the English Channel? They used tunnel-boring machines. These giant cylinders are as long as two football fields. The machines dug out 250 feet (76 meters) of the tunnel each day. That is like digging out a 20-story building.

The largest tunnel digging machine is called Bertha. Bertha is 57 feet (17.45 m) wide.

BUILDING WITH CYLINDERS

Cylinders form tall columns on buildings. These columns are called pillars. Some pillars help support the roof. Others decorate the building.

The U.S. Capitol Building in Washington, D.C., is famous for its columns. President George Washington chose the building's design. The original columns could not support the big iron dome on top of the Capitol. New columns were built. The old sandstone columns were set in a meadow with a reflecting pool. Now tourists can visit the National Capitol Columns.

There are 40 columns at the bottom of the U.S. Capitol's dome.

QUADRUPLE CYLINDERS

The BMW Tower in Germany is a skyscraper that has four cylinder-shaped towers. Builders fitted together the glass and steel tower on the ground. Then, they raised the towers 331 feet (101 m).

The BMW Tower's cylinders were designed to look like a car engine.

PIPES AND POLES

Other types of cylinders support or carry things. Pipes are shaped like cylinders. Copper, iron, and plastic pipes come in different widths. These pipes bring water and gases to our homes. Tall wood poles hold up power lines and cables. These wires carry electricity to our homes. They also bring us telephone service. The cylinder-shaped poles rise from 20 to 100 feet tall (6 to 30.5 m).

Most telephone poles weigh about 1,200 pounds (91 kilograms).

Long, skinny poles help people swing up and over a high crossbar. Athletes compete in a track and field event called pole vaulting. Who can clear the greatest height? That person wins the gold medal. Whoever wants to beat the world record for pole vaulting will need to leap higher than 20 feet (6 m).

The poles used by pole vaulters can be 10 to 17 feet long (3 to 5 m).

CYLINDERS IN NATURE

You can find cylinder shapes in nature. Many bamboo plants are shaped like cylinders. These plants grow quickly. Some bamboo can grow more than 3 feet (1 m) per day. In the desert, different types of **cacti** have cylinder shapes. Watch out, because they also have sharp spines.

There is a type of giant bamboo that can grow up to 164 feet (50 m) tall.

If you take a nature walk, you might discover a log that forms a perfect cylinder. You might glimpse a snake slithering through the grass, or you might discover worms wiggling beneath a rock. Both have cylinder-shaped bodies with no legs.

Be on the lookout for cylinders everywhere you go. It is amazing how many of these 3D shapes you can find outside, inside, and all around.

When cut, most tree trunks are cylinder-shaped.

CYLINDERS QUIZ

1 How much can some types of bamboo grow each day?

2 How many bases does a cylinder have?

3 What are three materials that pipes can be made out of?

4 What is the BMW Tower designed to look like?

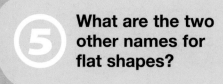

5 What are the two other names for flat shapes?

6 How many columns are at the bottom of the U.S. Capitol's dome?

7 What do the ripples on the side of a tin can do?

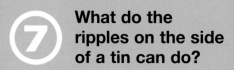

8 What is the world's largest tunnel digging machine called?

ACTIVITY:
MAKE A DRUM

Make this cylinder-shaped drum. Then, have fun drumming along to your favorite song.

Materials

- cylinder-shaped oatmeal container
- tape measure
- ruler
- pencil
- construction paper
- scissors
- glue stick
- yarn, glitter, stickers
- circle of waxed paper
- rubber band
- chopsticks or unsharpened pencils

Directions

1. Measure the dimensions of the oatmeal container using the tape measure.

2. Use the ruler and pencil to draw these measurements on the construction paper. Cut out the cylinder shape.

3. Glue the construction paper around the container.

4. Decorate your drum with yarn, glitter, and stickers.

5. Stretch the waxed paper circle over the open end of the container. Hold it in place with the rubber band.

6. Then, use chopsticks or unsharpened pencils as drumsticks. Drum on the waxed paper.

KEY WORDS

3D: a shape with length, width, and height

bases: the flat surfaces of a 3D shape

cacti: cactus plants

cylinders: 3D shapes with two flat circular bases and a curving round surface between them

dimensions: the length, width, or height of an object

faces: flat surfaces on a 3D shape

kaleidoscope: a tube-shaped toy with mirrors and pieces of colored glass or paper that produce patterns

reel: a cylinder on which flexible materials can be wound

rhythms: a repeated pattern of sound

surfaces: the flat or curved borders of a 3D shape

INDEX

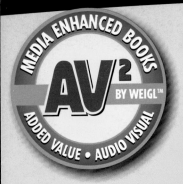

Log on to www.av2books.com

AV² by Weigl brings you media enhanced books that support active learning. Go to www.av2books.com, and enter the special code found on page 2 of this book. You will gain access to enriched and enhanced content that supplements and complements this book. Content includes video, audio, weblinks, quizzes, a slide show, and activities.

AV² Online Navigation

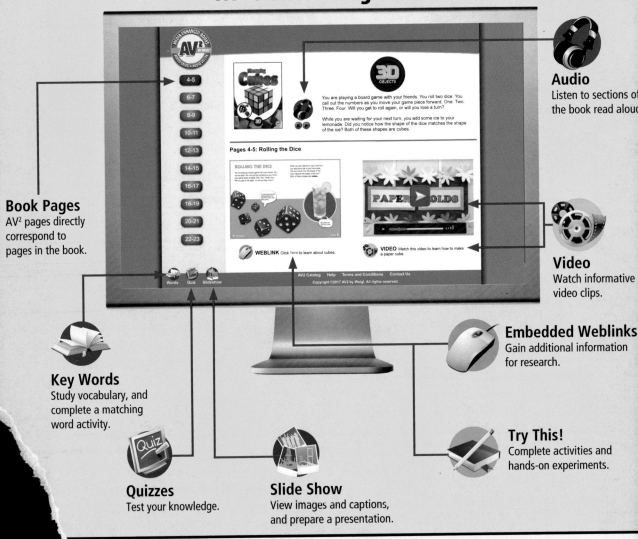

Book Pages
AV² pages directly correspond to pages in the book.

Audio
Listen to sections of the book read aloud.

Video
Watch informative video clips.

Key Words
Study vocabulary, and complete a matching word activity.

Embedded Weblinks
Gain additional information for research.

Try This!
Complete activities and hands-on experiments.

Quizzes
Test your knowledge.

Slide Show
View images and captions, and prepare a presentation.

AV² was built to bridge the gap between print and digital. We encourage you to tell us what you like and what you want to see in the future.

Sign up to be an AV² Ambassador at www.av2books.com/ambassador.

Due to the dynamic nature of the Internet, some of the URLs and activities provided as part of AV² by Weigl may have changed or ceased to exist. AV² by Weigl accepts no responsibility for any such changes. All media enhanced books are regularly monitored to update addresses and sites in a timely manner. Contact AV² by Weigl at 1-866-649-3445 or av2books@weigl.com with any questions, comments, or feedback.